Fables

Author: Natalie Hart
Editor: Elizabeth Goodwin

Frank Schaffer Publications®

Send all inquiries to:
Frank Schaffer Publications
8720 Orion Place
Columbus, Ohio 43240-2111

Lightning Lessons: Instant Units-Fables—grades 1-2

ISBN: 0-7682-3871-4

1 2 3 4 5 6 7 8 9 10 POH 12 11 10 09 08 07

Table of Contents

0-7682-3871-4 *Lightning Lessons: Fables*

Introduction to Lightning Lessons

This *Lightning Lesson* is a comprehensive unit that will support your instruction on story elements. The theme for this lesson is "Fables." In this unit, students will study and explore three familiar fables—Goldilocks and the Three Bears, The Little Red Hen, and The Three Little Pigs—as well as some of Aesop's fables.

Fables are an excellent way to teach about story elements. The fables chosen for this unit are well-known, making it that much easier for students to identify story elements in each fable. Students will study a traditional and alternative version of each story. They will compare the different versions of the stories using two graphic organizers: a story map and a Venn diagram. In addition to studying the basic story elements, students will also explore the *who, what, when, where,* and *why* of a story.

This unit contains daily journal writing prompts, connections to literature and technology, and suggestions for small group activities. The journal writing prompts will guide students through writing and illustrating their own animal fables. Students will also have the opportunity to create a fable as a class through the activities in the technology section. The *Lightning Words* are vocabulary words specific to the unit. Students can keep the list of words in their unit folder to refer to when necessary.

This *Lightning Lesson* also includes a story map poster you can laminate and use over and over as you explore with students the concepts of setting, characters, and story sequence.

You may wish to do this unit over the course of a week, a month, or even a whole year. The activities are flexible, with multiple options that allow you to adapt them to the specific needs and skill levels in your class. You may wish to try all the activities and projects over the course of a few months, or just choose your favorites for a shorter unit. An assessment checklist is included to help you keep track of your students' progress.

0-7682-3871-4 *Lightning Lessons: Fables*

Getting Started
Introducing the Lightning Unit to Your Students

Questions for Discussion
(using listening and speaking strategies, understanding literary genres)

When you are ready to get started, lead students in a discussion about fables. Ask students to name all the fables they can think of. Tell students that fables are stories that were originally passed down from person to person through the spoken word. Explain that fables teach about danger, give a moral lesson, or explain natural phenomena.

Books for Your Collection

There are a number of books about fables. These are just a few suggestions for traditional and alternative versions of popular fables:

- *Aesop's Fables* by Jerry Pinkney
- *Aesop Fables from Aesop* by Barbara McClintock
- *Dusty Locks and The Three Bears* by Susan Lowell
- *Fables from Aesop* by Tom Lynch
- *Goldie and the Three Bears* by Diane Stanley
- *Goldilocks and the Three Bears* by Jan Brett
- *Goldilocks and the Three Bears* by Candice Ransom
- *Goldilocks Returns* by Lisa Campbell Ernst
- *Learn to Read With Classic Stories, Grade 1* by American Education Publishing
- *Mr. Wolf and the Three Bears* by Jan Fearnley
- *Mr. Wolf's Pancakes* by Jan Fearnley
- *The Little Red Hen* by Carol Ottolenghi
- *The Little Red Hen: An Old Story* by Margot Zemach
- *The Little Red Hen (Makes a Pizza)* by Philemon Sturges
- *The Little Red Hen and the Ear of Wheat* by Mary Finch
- *The Three Pigs* by David Wiesner
- *Three Little Hawaiian Pigs and the Magic Shark* by Donivee Laird
- *The Three Little Pigs* by James Marshall
- *The Three Little Pigs* by Patricia Seibert
- *The Three Little Wolves and the Big Bad Pig* by Eugene Trivizas
- *The True Story of the Three Little Pigs by A. Wolf* by Jon Scieszka

0-7682-3871-4 *Lightning Lessons: Fables*

Lightning Resources
Connecting With Resources

Using the Poster
(identifying story elements, using story maps, comparing and contrasting, using graphic organizers)

Laminate the poster so that you can re-use it throughout the unit. Start by reading a traditional version of The Little Red Hen to your class, pointing out the title, author, setting, characters, beginning, middle, and end. Then, using a dry erase pen, fill in the story map poster as a class.

Next, read an alternative version of The Little Red Hen. Give each student a copy of the reproducible story map on page 24 for them to fill out individually. Put a comparison chart or Venn diagram on poster board or the chalkboard. Compare the two stories using the story map poster and the story maps the students completed.

You can use the poster and reproducible story map for any story. Repeat the activity above with Goldilocks and the Three Bears and The Three Little Pigs. Then, move on to other fables. As students become more acquainted with story elements, call them to the front to fill out portions of the story map poster. You can also complete the story map poster ahead of time for students to use as a self-check tool for the story maps they complete on their own.

Story Elements Reproducibles
(identifying, understanding, and using story elements)

The story elements worksheets on pages 11–22 help students learn about the elements of a story so that they can implement that knowledge into their own fables. First, students will learn about the *who, what, when, where,* and *why* of a story. Next, students will study characters and setting. Students can use the *Imagine Who* activity on page 14 to help them develop the characters that they want to include in the fables they are creating in their journals.

Story Map Reproducibles and Graphic Organizers
(identifying story elements, using a graphic organizer, comparing and contrasting)

Story Map Basics on page 23 gives students an introduction to creating story maps. Page 24 contains a reproducible version of the unit poster. This map is generic, so it can be used outside the unit as well. The story map on page 25 was designed to be used with any version of Goldilocks and The Three Bears.

Pages 26 and 27 contain more graphic organizers. These organizers will help students compare two fables and chart the differences and similarities.

Reading Comprehension Reproducibles
(reading comprehension, writing response)

Use the activities on pages 28–30 at anytime during the unit to test students' reading comprehension. The cloze activity starting on page 29 can be used over and over again, since the blanks within the story allow for multiple answers.

0-7682-3871-4 *Lightning Lessons: Fables*

Lightning Resources
Connecting With Resources

Connecting With Writing

(using skills and strategies of writing, using vocabulary, critical thinking, creative thinking, using a graphic organizer)

Use the instructions on this page and the template on page 10 to help your students create fable books about two animals. First, distribute copies of the story map on page 24. Instruct students to choose characters, a setting, a problem, and a solution for their fables and map them on their story maps. Students can do this as one activity, or focus on one story element each day. When the story maps are complete, pass out copies of the journal template on page 10. Write the prompts listed below on the chalkboard or whiteboard. Students will use the prompts and their story maps to create each page of their fable books. Again, students can complete all the prompts at once, or focus on a new prompt each day.

Page 1 prompt: *Write the title of your story on the lines at the bottom of your journal page.*
Then, draw the cover picture.

Page 2 prompt: *Write a sentence that tells the characters' names and where they live.*
Draw a picture to illustrate the sentence.

Page 3 prompt: *Write a sentence that describes the problem the characters have and how they feel about it.*
Draw a picture to illustrate the sentence.

Page 4 prompt: *Write a sentence that describes one way the characters try to solve the problem.*
Draw a picture to illustrate the sentence.

Page 5 prompt: *Write a sentence that tells why their first solution didn't work.*
Draw a picture to illustrate the sentence.

Page 6 prompt: *Write a sentence that describes another way the characters try to solve the problem.*
Draw a picture to illustrate the sentence.

Page 7 prompt: *Write a sentence that tells why their second solution worked.*
Draw a picture to illustrate the sentence.

Page 8 prompt: *Write a sentence that tells how the characters feel now that their problem is solved.*
Draw a picture to illustrate the sentence.

Published by Frank Schaffer Publications. Copyright protected. 0-7682-3871-4 *Lightning Lessons: Fables*

Lightning Resources

Name _____

Lightning Words

Date _____

author {AW-ther} the writer of a book, play, story, or other written work

character {KARE-ak-ter} a person or animal in a story

fable {FAY-bul} a story that teaches a lesson and in which the characters are animals who talk and act like people

illustrator {IL-uh-STRAY-ter} a person who draws or paints pictures for a book

setting {SET-ing} where and when a story takes place

story map {STOR-ee map} a form you can use to write down important facts about a story

title {TYE-tul} what a book is called or named

Venn diagram {ven DYE-uh-gram} a way to organize your thoughts when you have to compare two or more things

7

Lightning Connections
Connecting With Technology

Web Sites
(understanding story elements, understanding literary genres, using technology)

There are a number of Web sites you can access for story elements practice and materials related to fables.
- www.teachersdesk.com/lessons/esl/fables/Fables.htm features written versions of different fables along with corresponding activities for you to print or re-create.
- www.aesopfables.com features audio links to a number of fables. The site also offers several versions of each fable and some historical information about Aesop.
- www.readwritethink.org has a number of interactive language arts resources, including an interactive Venn diagram.

Cell Phone
(understanding literary genres, using listening and speaking strategies, understanding story elements, understanding technology, using a graphic organizer)

Play the traditional game Telephone, but call it "Cell Phone." Start the game by whispering a very short story to one student. The students will pass the story down using their "cell phones." Use a Venn diagram to compare the story you told with the story relayed at the end of the game.

PowerPoint Story
(understanding literary genres, using art to express ideas and feelings, applying visual arts, understanding story elements, using technology)

Use the text from a fable of your choice. Divide lines from the text among your students. Each student should illustrate a picture to go with his or her portion of the text. Scan the pictures to your classroom computer, and save them in sequential order in a file. Open Microsoft PowerPoint and select a illustration to go on each slide. Each student will type the text for his or her illustration on the correct slide. When the PowerPoint is complete, watch it as a class. You can also save the presentation and show it during an open house.

8

Lightning Connections
Connecting With Arts and Literature

Story Telling
(using listening and speaking strategies, identifying story elements)

Demonstrate the origins of fables to your students by bringing a storyteller to the class. Ask your students to pay careful attention to the characters and different parts of the story as they listen. The National Storytelling Network's Web site has a directory of storytellers in your area. Visit the site at www.storynet.org, or contact the Network at 1-800-525-4514.

Painting a Story
(using art to express ideas and feelings, applying media, techniques, and processes of the visual arts, understanding art in relation to history and culture)

The book *Aesop's Fables* by Jerry Pinkney is full of illustrations from the well-known illustrator. Show your students a few of the paintings. Explain that Mr. Pinkney used watercolors and colored pencils to create illustrations to accompany the stories in the book. Ask your students which pictures they like the best and why.

Tell each student to choose a fable to illustrate. Then, pass out watercolor paints, colored pencils, and watercolor paper (available at any arts and crafts store) and have students paint pictures to accompany their chosen fables.

Fable Theater
(identifying story elements, understanding conventions of media, summarizing, using skills and strategies of writing)

Watch Aesop's fables on the big screen! *Aesop's Fables, Volume 1* by East West Entertainment features several fun, G-rated shorts. Make popcorn and have students bring in pillows for a relaxed movie experience. Afterward, have students write a summary about one of the stories in the movie.

Extra, Extra! Read All About It!
(understanding story elements, using skills and strategies of writing, understanding characteristics and components of newspapers)

Use publishing software, like Microsoft Publisher, to create a newspaper template. Give students a fable to use as a writing prompt, and have them re-write the fable as a news story. Show students page 13 as an example. This is a good opportunity to discuss the *who, what, when, where,* and *why* of a story. Type the news stories and add them to the newspaper template. Make enough copies of your classroom newspaper for each student to have one.

Published by Frank Schaffer Publications. Copyright protected.   0-7682-3871-4 *Lightning Lessons: Fables*

Lightning Activities

Name _____

My Fable Journal

Date _____

_____

_____

_____

_____

0-7682-3871-4 *Lightning Lessons: Fables*

Lightning Activities

Name _____

Flying Ws

Date _____

(understanding story elements, reading comprehension)

Read a fable, then answer the Flying W questions.

WHO is this fable about?

_____

WHERE does this fable happen?

_____

WHEN does this fable happen?

_____

WHAT is this fable about?

_____

0-7682-3871-4 *Lightning Lessons: Fables*

Lightning Activities

Name _____

The Three Little Pigs

Date _____

(understanding story elements, reading comprehension)

Read a version of The Three Little Pigs. Then, ask the questions a reporter asks: *Who? What? When? Where? Why?* Fill in the blanks below.

Title: _____

Author: _____

Who is in the story? _____

_____

What happens first? _____

_____

What happens last? _____

_____

What is the problem in the story? _____

_____

When does the story take place? _____

Where does the story take place? _____

Why do the characters have a problem? _____

_____

0-7682-3871-4 *Lightning Lessons: Fables*

Lightning Activities

Name _____

News Story

Date _____

(understanding story elements, reading comprehension, understanding informational texts)

Read the newspaper story. Then, answer the questions.

Girl Breaks into the Bear Family House

by I. M. Furry

The Bear family went on a walk yesterday. They were gone for a short time when a young girl broke into their house.

"It was awful," cried Mother Bear. "She ate our food. She sat in our chairs! She even slept in our beds!"

The police asked many questions. It seems that the girl broke Baby Bear's chair. The police are looking for a little girl with blond hair. She goes by the name of Goldilocks. The neighbors are asked to lock their doors and watch carefully for any strangers along the road.

1. Who is the news story about?

_____

_____

2. What is the news story about?
    A. the Bear Family's walk
    B. Goldilocks breaking into the Bear Family's house
    C. little girls with blonde hair

3. Why are the police looking for Goldilocks?

_____

_____

13

0-7682-3871-4 *Lightning Lessons: Fables*

Lightning Activities

Name _____

Date _____

Imagine Who

(exploring characters)

Characters are the people or animals in a story.
Draw a picture of a character you would like to tell a story about.
Then, answer the questions about your character.

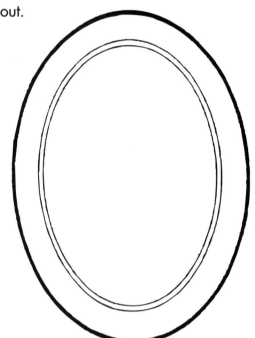

1. What is your character's name?

_____

2. What does he or she look like?

_____

3. What are your character's favorite things to do?

_____

4. What makes your character happy?

_____

5. What makes your character sad or scared?

_____

0-7682-3871-4 *Lightning Lessons: Fables*

Lightning Activities

Alike and Different

Name _____

Date _____

(exploring characters, comparing and contrasting, reading comprehension)

Read a story about City Mouse and Country Mouse. Draw a line to the mouse the words tell about. If the words tell about both mice, draw a line to both of them.

lives in a garden

has a cousin

eats cookies

eats vegetables

lives in a fancy house

is afraid of dogs

15

0-7682-3871-4 *Lightning Lessons: Fables*

Lightning Activities

Two Little Pigs

Name _____

Date _____

(using skills and strategies of reading)

Read the story.

Once upon a time, there were two little pigs. They lived with their mother in the city. The two little pigs wanted to live in the country. They could plant a garden in the country. They would make new animal friends, too.

When they kissed their mother good-bye, she said, "Watch out for the wolf. Little pigs are his favorite snack."

The pigs walked until they found a pile of sticks. "I'm tired of walking. I will build a house with these sticks," said the first little pig. And he did.

The second little pig walked on until he saw a pile of stones. "I will build my house of stones and mud," he said, "because it will be strong."

When the hungry wolf heard about the two pigs, he said, "This is great! Pigs are my favorite snack food." He blew down the first pig's house with one huff because the stick house was not strong. The first little pig ran to his brother's house.

"Brother, I have never been so scared in my life!" said the first little pig.

"Don't worry," said the second little pig. "I think we will be safe."

The second little pig was right. The wolf went home hungry that day. "It's not fair that pigs can build stone houses!" he said to himself.

0-7682-3871-4 *Lightning Lessons: Fables*

Lightning Activities

Name _____

Two Little Pigs (cont.)

Date _____

(exploring characters, reading comprehension)

Each statement could have been said by one of the characters in the story on page 16.
Circle the name of the character that might have said each statement.

1. "I am tired of walking."

   First Little Pig   **Second Little Pig**   **Wolf**

2. "A house of sticks will be strong enough."

   First Little Pig   **Second Little Pig**   **Wolf**

3. "Pigs are my favorite snack food."

   First Little Pig   **Second Little Pig**   **Wolf**

4. "A stone house will be strong."

   First Little Pig   **Second Little Pig**   **Wolf**

5. "Pigs should not be allowed to build stone houses."

   First Little Pig   **Second Little Pig**   **Wolf**

6. "I have never been so scared in my life!"

   First Little Pig   **Second Little Pig**   **Wolf**

7. "I think we will be safe in the stone house."

   First Little Pig   **Second Little Pig**   **Wolf**

8. "I will never build a house out of sticks again."

   First Little Pig   **Second Little Pig**   **Wolf**

17

0-7682-3871-4 *Lightning Lessons: Fables*

Lightning Activities

Name _____

Characters

Date _____

(comparing and contrasting, using a graphic organizer, reading comprehension)

Choose two characters from one book and compare them.

What is the character's name?		
What does this character look like?		
What words does the author use to describe this character?		
What words would you use to describe this character?		
If this character has a saying, what is it?		
What do other characters think about this character?		
Does this character have a happy ending or a sad ending?		

0-7682-3871-4 *Lightning Lessons: Fables*

Lightning Activities

Aesop's Lessons

Name _____

Date _____

(exploring characters, reading comprehension)

Read versions of The Tortoise and the Hare, City Mouse, Country Mouse, and The Lion and the Mouse. Then, draw a line from the lesson to the character who learned the lesson.

The Hare

• It is better to eat a simple meal in peace than to eat a feast in fear.

The Country Mouse

• Sometimes, small friends can be big helpers.

The Lion

• Slow and steady wins the race.

0-7682-3871-4 *Lightning Lessons: Fables*

Lightning Activities

Dear Character

(exploring characters)

Write a letter to your favorite fable character.

Dear _____,

I like to read about you in _____.

My favorite part of the story is _____

_____.

If I were you, I would _____

_____.

Sincerely,

_____

Published by Frank Schaffer Publications. Copyright protected.   0-7682-3871-4 *Lightning Lessons: Fables*

Lightning Activities

Name _____

Date _____

Setting

(understanding and identifying setting)

A **setting** is where a story takes place.

Imagine a snowy place.
Draw a picture of your "snowy setting."

Write a sentence describing your snowy setting.

_____

Imagine a sunny place.
Draw a picture of your "sunny setting."

Write a sentence describing your sunny setting.

_____

21

Lightning Activities

Name _____

Setting—Time

Date _____

(understanding and identifying setting)

The **setting** is the **place** where the story happens. The setting is also the **time** in which the story happens. A reader needs to know **when** the story is happening. Does it take place at night? On a sunny day? In the future? During the winter?

Time can be:

time of day

a holiday

a season of the year

a time in history

a time in the future

Read the following story. Then, answer the questions below.

 **Pancake Mornings**

In the summer, I look forward to Sunday mornings. On Sundays, my parents get up extra early. My mom mixes pancake batter with ripe blueberries, and my dad plays the fiddle. When my brother and I come downstairs for breakfast, the pancakes are on the griddle and my dad is dancing!

1. On what day of the week does this story take place? _____

2. What season is it in this story? _____

3. What time of day is it? _____

22

Lightning Activities

Name _____

Story Map Basics

Date _____

(understanding story elements, sequencing, creating a basic story map)

A **story map** is like an outline.

This outline is all mixed up! Number the sentences from **1** to **7** to put them in order.

_____ First, she jumped up and down in the nest.

_____ Cleo felt herself rising.

_____ She was high above the nest.

_____ Cleo was flying!

_____ Cleo was a very small bird.

_____ Then, she opened her wings and flapped.

_____ She wanted to fly.

Now, write your own story map about what happens to Cleo next.

1. _____

2. _____

3. _____

4. _____

5. _____

23

Lightning Activities

Name _____

Story Map

Date _____

(identifying and understanding story elements, using a graphic organizer)

Title	Author

Setting	Characters

Beginning	Middle	End

0-7682-3871-4 *Lightning Lessons: Fables*

Lightning Activities

Name _____

Goldilocks and the Three Bears Story Map

Date _____

(identifying story elements, reading comprehension, organizing information)

Read a version of Goldilocks and the Three Bears. Then, fill in the story elements below.

Title: _____

_____

Author: _____

_____

Setting: _____

_____

Characters: _____

_____

_____

_____

Beginning

Middle

End

25

0-7682-3871-4 *Lightning Lessons: Fables*

Lightning Activities

Name _____

Comparing Stories

Date _____

(using a graphic organizer, identifying story elements, comparing and contrasting, reading comprehension)

Fill in the blanks to compare a traditional fable with an alternative version. Then, answer the questions at the bottom of the page.

Title		
Author		
Illustrator		
Setting		
Main Characters		
Which character causes trouble for the other characters?		
Which character has a happy ending?		
List one thing that is the same.		
List one thing that is different.		

Which story do you like best? _____

Why? _____

_____

_____

0-7682-3871-4 *Lightning Lessons: Fables*

Lightning Activities

Name _____

Venn Diagram

Date _____

(using a graphic organizer, comparing and contrasting)

Use this diagram to compare two things. (For example, compare two books, two characters, or two endings.) On the lines, write what you are comparing. In the middle shape, write what is true of both things. In the left circle, write things that are true of one thing. In the right circle, write things that are true of the other thing.

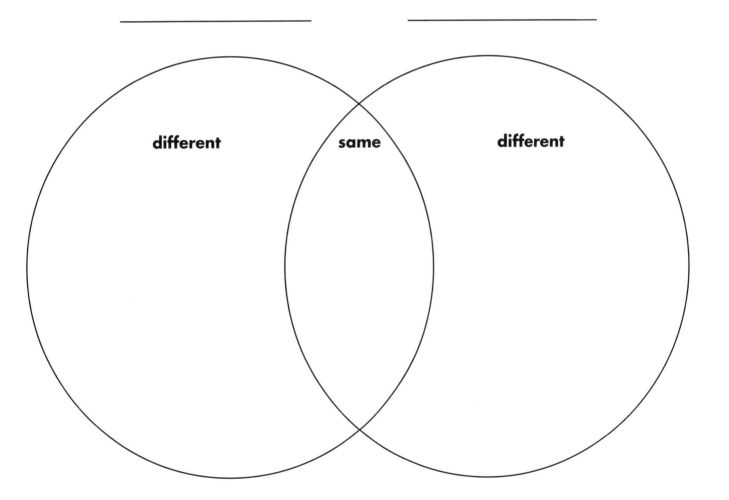

27

0-7682-3871-4 *Lightning Lessons: Fables*

Lightning Activities

Name _____

Reading Comprehension: Aesop's *The Fox and the Grapes*

Date _____

(reading comprehension, writing response)

Read the fable. Then, answer the questions.

A fox was walking through the woods when he saw some big, juicy grapes growing on a tall vine. "They look so delicious," he thought. "I think I will eat some of them for lunch."

The fox stood on his back legs to pick the grapes, but the grapes were much too high for the fox to reach. So, he stretched out his paw as far as he could. Still the fox could not reach the grapes. So he jumped as high as he could. The fox tried again and again, but he still could not reach the grapes. Finally, the fox gave up and walked away. "Who wants to eat those sour old grapes anyway?" he asked himself.

1. Is this story real or make-believe? How do you know?

   _____

   _____

2. How did the fox feel about the grapes at the beginning of the fable?

   _____

   Underline the sentence above that tells this.

3. Why did the fox say the grapes were sour at the end of the fable?
   A. because the grapes tasted bad
   B. because the grapes were too easy to pick
   C. because he was angry that he could not reach the grapes

4. Why did the author write this fable?
   A. to tell about the kinds of foods a fox will eat
   B. to entertain you with a story
   C. to make you feel sorry for the fox

28

Lightning Activities

Name _____

Change the Story: Goldilocks and the Three Bears   Date _____

(writing response, reading comprehension)

Fill in the blanks in the story below. Use your imagination! It is up to you to say how the story ends!

Goldilocks and the Three Bears, by _____
Your Name

Once upon a time, three bears lived in _____. Papa Bear was huge, Mama Bear was
The City Where You Live

big, and Baby Bear was teeny tiny. One morning, Mama Bear made _____ for breakfast,
Type of Food

but it was too hot to eat. The bears went for a walk in the _____ while the food cooled.
Place

While they were out, a little girl named Goldilocks walked by their house. She smelled the

_____. It smelled wonderful! She wanted to get in the house, so she _____
Type of Food

_____.
Describe How She Gets in the House

She tasted the _____ from the huge bowl. It was too hot! She tasted the
Type of Food

_____ from the big bowl. It was too cold! She tasted the _____ from the
Type of Food Type of Food

teeny, tiny bowl. Yum! It was just right, and she gobbled it all up.

Goldilocks was feeling _____, so she went to sit down in the living room. There was a
A Feeling

huge chair, a big chair, and a teeny, tiny chair. The huge chair was too hard, and the big chair was too

soft, but the teeny, tiny chair was just right. Oh no! Goldilocks _____ and the chair broke!
Action Word

Now, Goldilocks felt _____, so she went upstairs to lie down. The beds looked so good!
A Feeling

The huge bed was too hard. The big bed was too soft. But, the teeny, tiny bed was perfect! She fell

fast asleep.

0-7682-3871-4 *Lightning Lessons: Fables*

Lightning Activities

Change the Story: Goldilocks and the Three Bears (cont.)

The three bears came back from their walk in the _____. "Someone's been
                                                    Place

eating my _____!" roared Papa Bear. "Someone's been eating my _____,"
          Type of Food   Type of Food

said Mama Bear. "Someone's been eating my _____," squeaked Baby Bear. "And it's
                                          Type of Food

all gone!"

The bears went into the living room. "Someone's been sitting in my chair!" roared Papa Bear.

"Someone's been sitting in my chair," said Mama Bear. "Someone's been sitting in my chair," squeaked

Baby Bear. "And now it's broken!"

The bears went upstairs. "Someone was in my bed!" roared Papa Bear. "Someone was in my bed,"

said Mama Bear. "Someone was in my bed," squeaked Baby Bear. "And she's still there!"

Just then, Goldilocks opened her eyes. _____
                                               Write What Happens Next

_____

_____

_____

_____

Congratulations! You did it!

0-7682-3871-4 *Lightning Lessons: Fables*

Lightning Assessment
Answer Key

Page 11
Answers may vary.

Page 12
Answers may vary.

Page 13
1. The Bear Family, Goldilocks
2. B
3. because she broke into the Bear Family's house

Page 14
Answers may vary.

Page 15
Draw a line to connect these phrases to the City Mouse:
has a cousin
eats cookies
lives in a fancy house
is afraid of dogs

Draw a line to connect these phrases to the Country Mouse:
lives in a garden
has a cousin
eats vegetables
is afraid of dogs

Page 17
1. First Little Pig
2. First Little Pig
3. Wolf
4. Second Little Pig
5. Wolf
6. First Little Pig
7. Second Little Pig
8. First Little Pig

Page 18
Answers may vary.

Page 19
Connect The Hare to: "Slow and steady wins the race."
Connect The Country Mouse to: "It is better to eat a simple meal in peace than to eat a feast in fear."
Connect The Lion to: "Sometimes, small friends can be big helpers."

Page 20
Answers may vary.

Page 21
Answers may vary.

Page 22
1. Sunday
2. summer
3. morning

Page 23
3
5
6
7
1
4
2

Story maps may vary.

Page 24
Answers may vary.

Page 25
Answers may vary.

Page 26
Answers may vary.

Page 27
Answers may vary.

Page 28
1. make-believe; Animals do not talk in real life.
2. He thought the grapes would be good to eat.
3. C
4. B

Pages 29–30
Answers may vary.

0-7682-3871-4 *Lightning Lessons: Fables*

Lightning Assessment
Fables Unit Assessment Rubric

Name of Student _____

Skill	Consistently (3)	Sometimes (2)	Rarely (1)	Points
Imaginatively engaged with the material through journal				
Sentences were complete with full punctuation				
Sentences were legible with good word spacing				
Illustrations appropriately reflected the story				
Graphic organizers: information was clear, legible, and in the right spot				
Responded appropriately to comedic or dramatic moments in story				
Identified similarities and differences				
Identified beginning, middle, and end of a story				
Identified setting and characters in a story				
Identified problems and solutions in a story				
Worked independently in a timely manner				
Contributed to small group work				

Total: _____

Comments (include story elements with which the student needs more practice): _____
_____
_____
_____

0-7682-3871-4 *Lightning Lessons: Fables*